Stanton's Trilobite Primer

OR,
AN ABC'S OF TRILOBITES

STANTON F. FINK

Acknowledgments

and Dedication

To my father, in whose books I discovered my first monsters.

To Will Caligan, whose help and encouragement is one of the primary reasons for this coloring book's existence.

To Mariano Silvera, who should have had his own artbooks

To Doctor David Morafka, who helped teach me to be more picky with my information.

To my friends, who helped push me to make this.

Table of Contents

Introduction

The purpose of this coloring book series is to provide information on various prehistoric animals both profoundly famous and incredibly obscure to artists of all ages. Of course, there is a lot of material to work with, as animals have been a major component of Earth's ecosystems for at least 670 million years.

If you, or your inner and or outer child do not see your favorite prehistoric animal here, it may be eventually featured in another volume. Or, contact me to have it put into a later volume.

Trilobites are probably the secondmost iconic group of fossil animals after the non-avian dinosaurs. Trilobites lasted about 270 million years, from the Early Cambrian, 521 million years ago, until the end of the Permian 250 million years ago. Although the most primitive known trilobites appear 521 million years ago, that they are already complicated creatures with a worldwide distribution strongly suggests that the ancestral trilobite still remains hidden in the vicissitudes of time and tectonic movements.

During the first half of the Paleozoic, trilobites formed important groups in their respective ecosystems. By the time the Late Devonian Extinction Event came, all trilobites went extinct, save for the Proetids, who continued to persist in marine ecosystems until the very last of them died out by the Permian Triassic Extinction Event.

Humans value trilobites partly for the insights trilobites provide about evolutionary biology in general, and about life in Paleozoic marine environments in particular, and partly for their peculiar, anciently arcane appearances.

Glossary

- **Aquatic**- Living in water.
- **Arthropod**- Any member of the animal phylum Arthropoda, including trilobites, arachnids, crustaceans, insects, myriapods and their relatives. All arthropods have armor-like, jointed exoskeletons made of chitin-derived plates, sometimes reinforced with calcium carbonate, and jointed limbs.
- **Cambrian**- A period of time in the Paleozoic Era from 541 to 485 million years ago.
- **Carboniferous**- A period of time in the Paleozoic Era from 359 to 300 million years ago.
- **Cephalon**- The shield-like structure which formed the head of the trilobite.
- **Chelicerate**- Any member of the arthropod subphylum Chelicerata, and include the arachnids, eurypterids or sea scorpions, and the horseshoe crabs. The chelicerates are thought to be descendants of one of the many minor groups of primitive arthropods from the Cambrian that looked too suspiciously like trilobites, possibly the aglaspids
- **Chordate**- Any member of the animal phylum Chordata, including sea squirts, lancet fish, and vertebrates (such as lampreys, sharks, tuna, frogs, lizards, chickens, and people). All chordates have, at least at some point in their life cycle, a notochord, a long, flexible rod, usually made of cartilage, or, in the case of most vertebrates, cartilage and bone, running down the back from head to tail, directly beneath the neural tube.
- **Devonian**- A period of time in the Paleozoic Era from 414 to 360 million years ago.
- **Ediacaran**- The last period of time in the Precambrian Eon from 635 to 542 million years ago.
- **Fauna**- In an ecological context, "fauna" refers to the animal components of an ecosystem.
- **Formation**- In a geological or paleontological context, a formation is a group of rock layers.
- **Glabellum**- A nose-like, or dome-like structure in the center of the cephalon between the eyes. The glabellum is located above the mouth, and served as a stomach-like storage chamber to hold swallowed food. Plural is "glabella."
- **Mollusk**- Any member of the animal phylum Mollusca, including snails, clams, squid, octopuses, tusk shells and chitons. Most mollusks have a calcium carbonate shell, and a toothed, file-like tongue called a radula. All mollusks have a cape-like organ, the mantle, which usually secretes the shell, and houses breathing organs, and a nervous system.
- **Nekton**- Any aquatic animal that lives either entirely or almost entirely in the water column, and relies on its own swimming or propulsion abilities to keep and move itself in and around the water column. Anchovies, porpoises and ichthyosaurs are examples of nekton.
- **Ordovician**- A period of time in the Paleozoic Era from 484 to 440 million years ago.

- **Paleozoic**- An era of time in the Phanerozoic Eon from 249 to 66 million years ago.
- **Permian**- The last period of time in the Paleozoic Era, the time of "The Great Dying," or most severe of all known extinction events, from 299 to 250 million years ago.
- **Plankton**- An organism that uses water currents and waterflow to as its primary means of transportation in the water column because it is either too small to move long distances by its own power, or lacks the ability to propel itself entirely. Sargassum seaweed and jellyfish are two varieties of plankton.
- **Pygidium**- The last, posteriormost segments of the trilobite which are fused together to form a shield-like structure. Plural is "pygidia."
- **Silurian**- A period of time in the Paleozoic Era from 440 to 419 million years ago.
- **Terrestrial**- Living on land.
- **Thorax**- The central segments which form the body of the trilobite, between the cephalon and the pygidium: most trilobites had an average of nine to eleven thoracic segments, though some dwarf trilobites, such as the agnostids, had as few as two, while some others had as many as twenty. Plural is "thoraces."

A is for *Afrops larvifer*

Phylum	Arthropoda
Class	Trilobita
Order	Phacopida
Family	Phacopidae
Subfamily	Phacopidellinae
Size	Holotype and only known specimen, an incomplete cephalon, about 2 centimeters long.
Time Period	Pragian Epoch of the Early Devonian, 407 to 410 million years ago
Location	Southwestern Algeria
Comments	*Afrops larvifer* is a blind phacopid trilobite from a diverse community of trilobites in what is now the southwestern portion of Algeria.

Afrops larvifer is a blind phacopid trilobite from a diverse community of trilobites in what is now the southwestern portion of Algeria.

Phacopids are best known for having evolved complex compound eyes, termed "schizochroal" eyes, where each individual eye had its own corneal wall. Having said that, several phacopid genera, including *Afrops, Ductina* and *Cryphops,* evolved reduced eyes or dispensed with them entirely, becoming blind. Each visually reduced or eyeless genus would have its own evolutionary reasons or constraints for becoming as such, like living in a low-visibility or lightless environment, or, possibly, with the case of *A. larvifer,* whose neighboring trilobites had well-developed eyes, taking up a burrowing lifestyle.

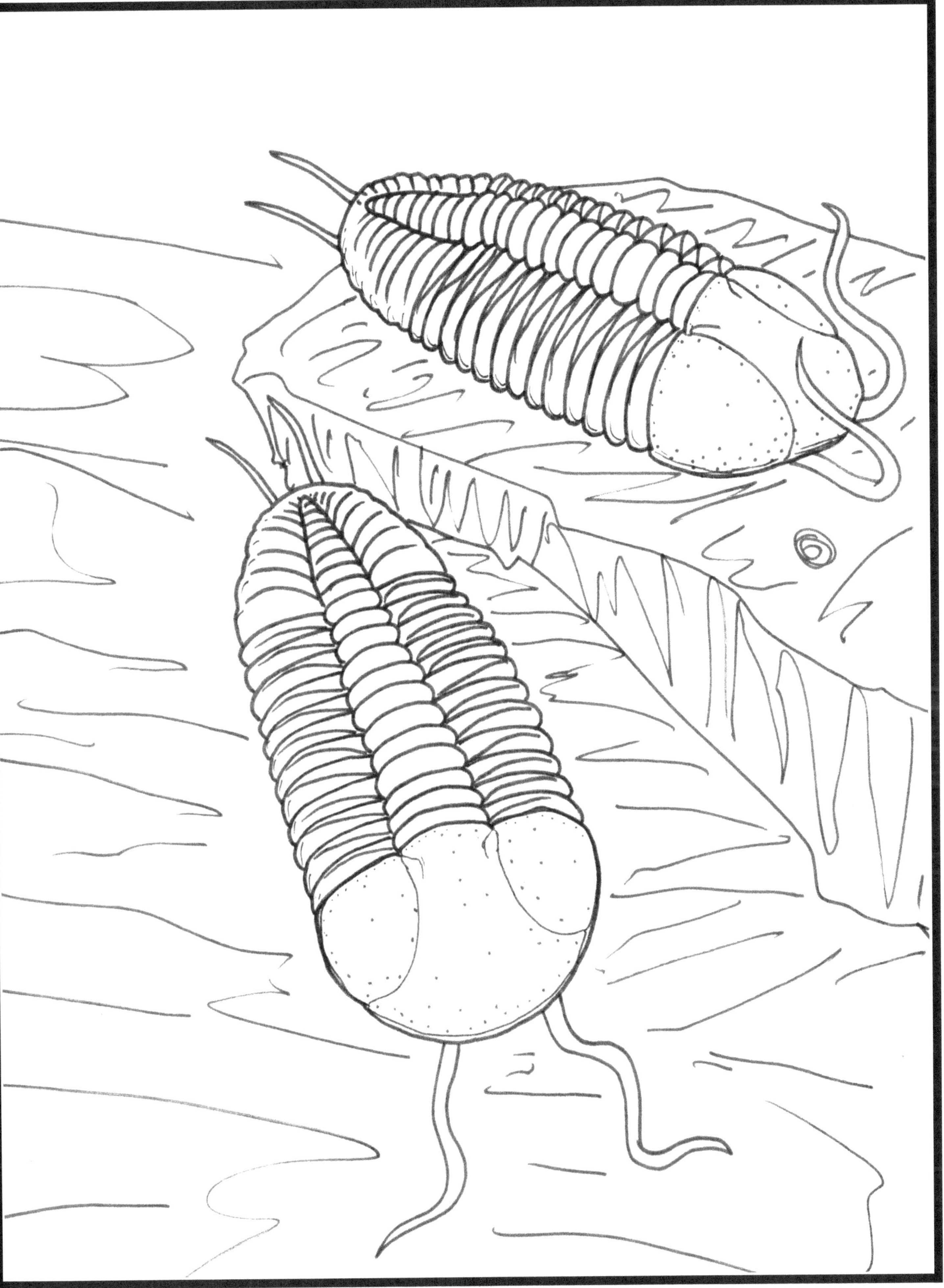

B is for *Biceratops nevadensis*

Phylum Arthropoda

Class Trilobita

Order Redlichiida

Family Biceratopsidae

Size Body average length about 8 centimeters without pleural spines or pygidium

Time Period Toyonian Stage of the Early Cambrian Period, 513 to 516 million years ago

Location Pioche Shale of the Frenchman Mountain, Clark County, Nevada

Comments *Biceratops nevadensis* is a redlichiid trilobite from what is now the American state of Nevada, where it lived in a shallow marine environment together with the related genera *Olenellus,* and *Mesonacis.*

B. nevadensis is named for its pair of enormously prominent pleural spines that suggest horns. *Biceratops* has no genal spines (spines that emanate from the corners, or cheeks of the cephalon), though, all of its other close relatives, such as *Peachella* and *Emigrantia,* do.

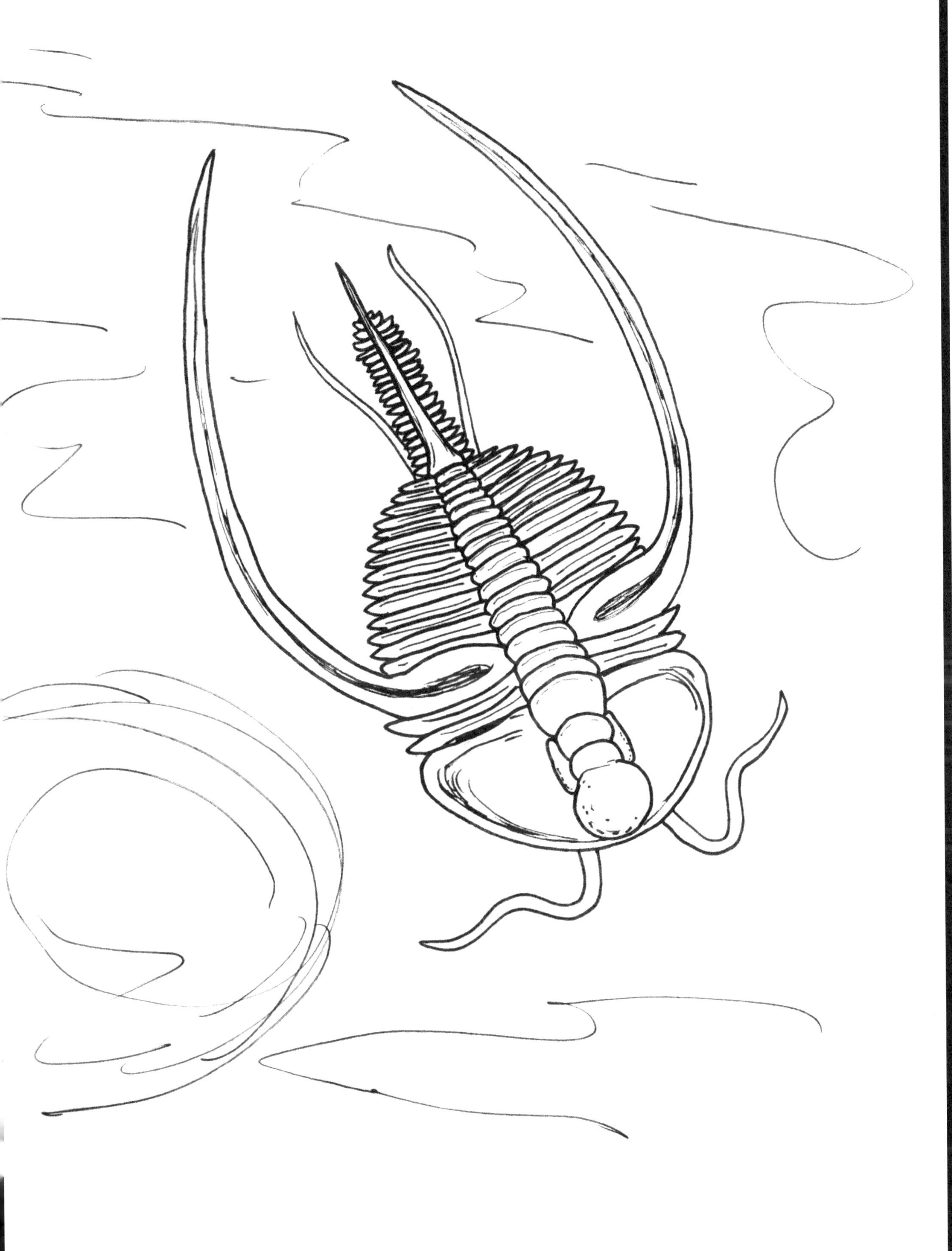

C is for   *Chamaeleoaspis chamaeleo*

Phylum	Arthropoda
Class	Trilobita
Order	Proetida
Family	Aulacopleuridae
Size	Bodylength, without spines, about 3 millimeters
Time Period	Middle Eifelian Epoch of the Middle Devonian, about 393 million years ago
Location	Ohle Formation in Endorf, Germany
Comments	*Chamaeleoaspis chamaeleo* is a tiny proetid trilobite from the Middle Devonian. Its scientific name alludes to the situations of how it, and its sister species from Morocco, *C. ikomalii*, are very similar to the related genera *Cyphaspis* and *Otarionella*, and how both species were successively classified within both other genera before being put into their own genus. Effectively, the generic name commemorates how *C. chamaeleo* and *C. ikomalii* are taxonomically chameleonic. Of course, humans would probably have a difficult time detecting the living animals, as fossils of *Chamaeleoaspis* suggest that, even with their awe-filled phalanx of spines, living individuals would have been slightly more than half a centimeter in length.

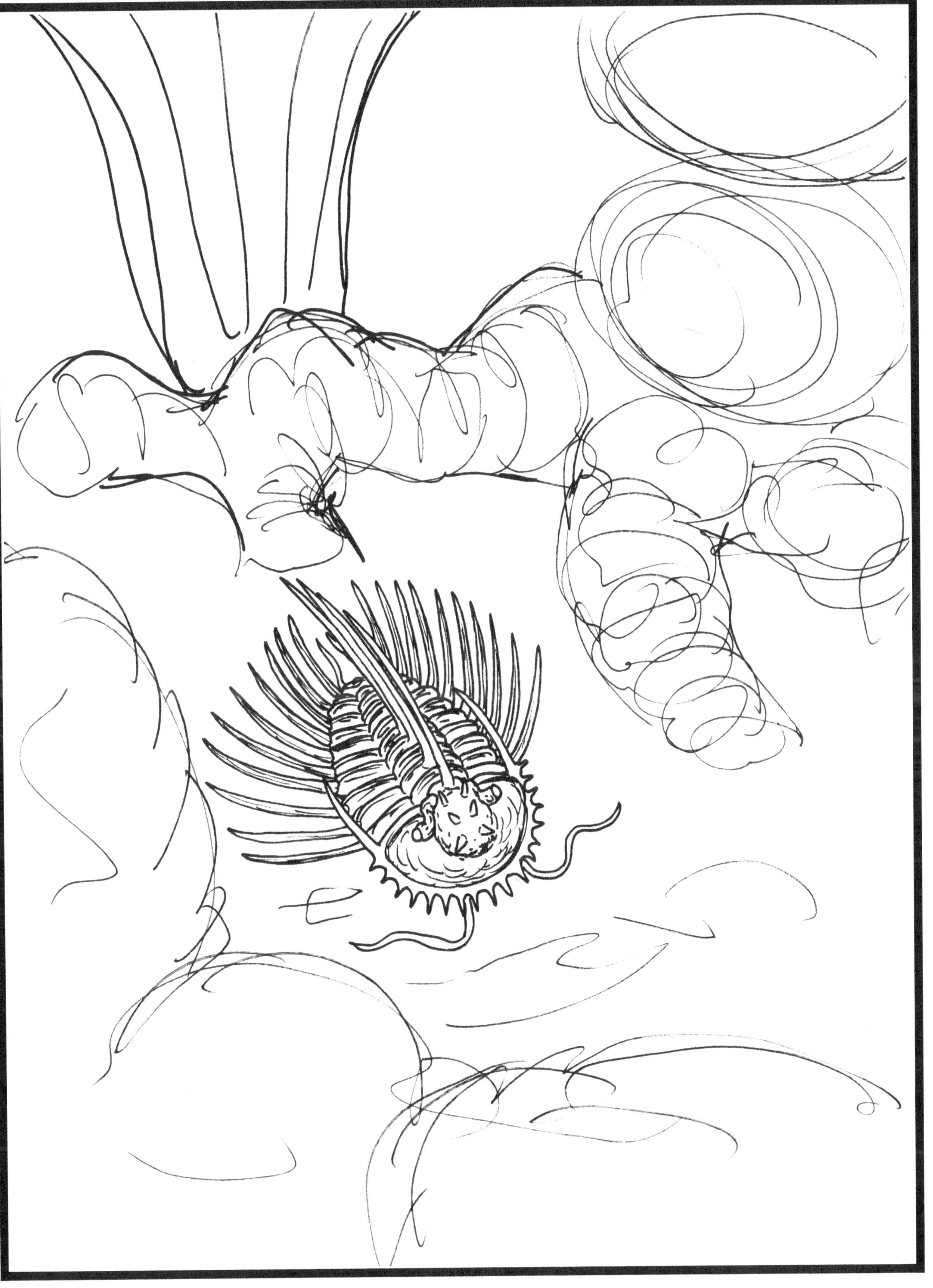

D is for *Dicranurus monstrosus*

Phylum	Arthropoda
Class	Trilobita
Order	Odontopleurida
Family	Odontopleuridae
Size	Up to 6 centimeters in length and width with spines, body length without spines about 2 to 2.5 centimeters.
Time Period	Late Pragian to Early Emsian epochs of the Middle Devonian, 408 to 395 million years ago
Location	Morocco and Bohemia
Comments	The extravagantly horned *Dicranurus monstrosus* is probably the most famous odontopleurid trilobite, as its iconic, curling head-horns for which the genus is named are unmistakable.

In the case of *D. monstrosus*, the horns are the largest, most-curving in the genus. The horns' purpose are, as with the spines of all fabulously spinose trilobites, the source of much speculation. The most plausible hypothesis states that the lateral spines helped redistributed the animal's weight so that it would not sink into soft mud, while both the lateral and head spines discouraged gnathostome vertebrate predators, such as the arthrodire placoderm, *Atlantidosteus*, shown here.

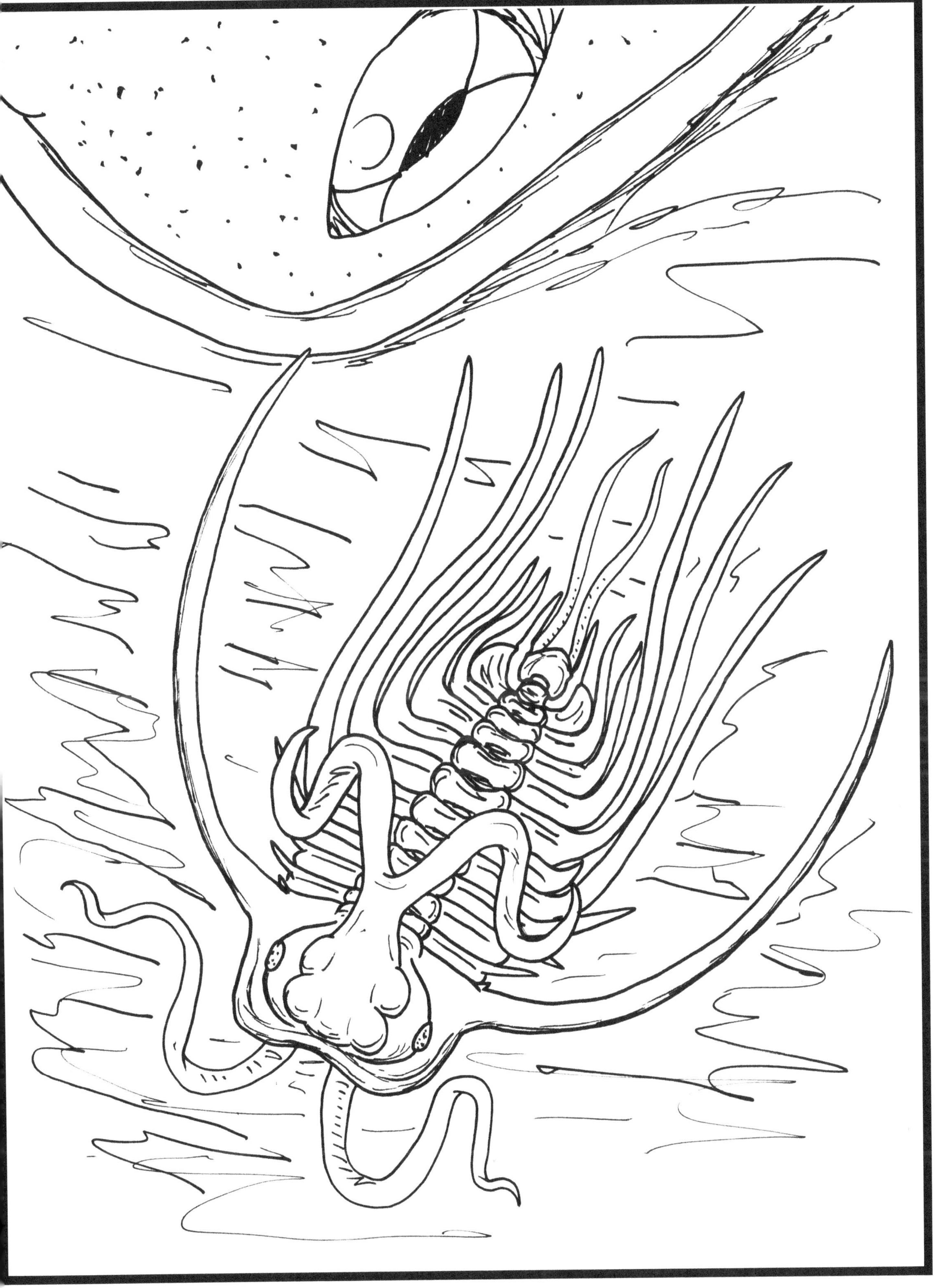

E is for *Endops yanagisamai*

Phylum	Arthropoda
Class	Trilobita
Order	Proetida
Family	Phillipsiidae
Size	Around 3 to 4 centimeters
Time Period	Late Capitanian Epoch, Middle Permian Period about 260 million years ago.
Location	Takakura Formation, Abukuma Mountains, Fukushima Prefecture, Honshu Island, Japan

Comments

During the Permian Period, in the twilight of the trilobites, there were still localities where trilobites remained or became diverse in species, such as in Texas, Oman, China, and in the case of *Endops yanagisamai* (originally described as "*Paladin*" *yanagisamai*), Japan.

In Permian Japan, there were several species of proetids from the families Proetidae, Phillipsiidae, and Brachymetopidae: most of these species were of worldwide distribution. *Endops* was endemic, but, the ironically named genus *Nipponaspis* (meaning "Japan's shield") had several species found in Permian China as well as a species in Japan that coexisted with *E. yanagisamai*.

F is for *Fritzaspis generalis*

Phylum	Arthropoda
Class	Trilobita
Order	Redlichiida
Family	Archaeaspididae
Size	Cephalon about 2 centimeters wide
Time Period	Early part of Atdabanian Stage of the Early Cambrian Period, about 521 million years ago.
Location	Esmeralda County, Nevada
Comments	*Fritzaspis generalis* is the most common trilobite in the oldest known trilobite community from what was once the coast of the Cambrian-aged continet of Laurentia, hence "*generalis.*" *F. generalis* and its rarer sister species, *F. ovalis* are named in honor of paleontologist W. H. Fritz, who found the first specimens. *Fritzaspis* is very similar to the older *Repinaella*, from what is now Morocco, and may be an ancestor of the younger, and more prominently spined *Archaeaspis*, which has species in Siberia and California. While *F. generalis* was the most common trilobite in this brachiopod-dominated environment, trilobites were very rare in that region, with about a half dozen to a dozen specimens of *F. generalis* found throughout Esmeralda County.

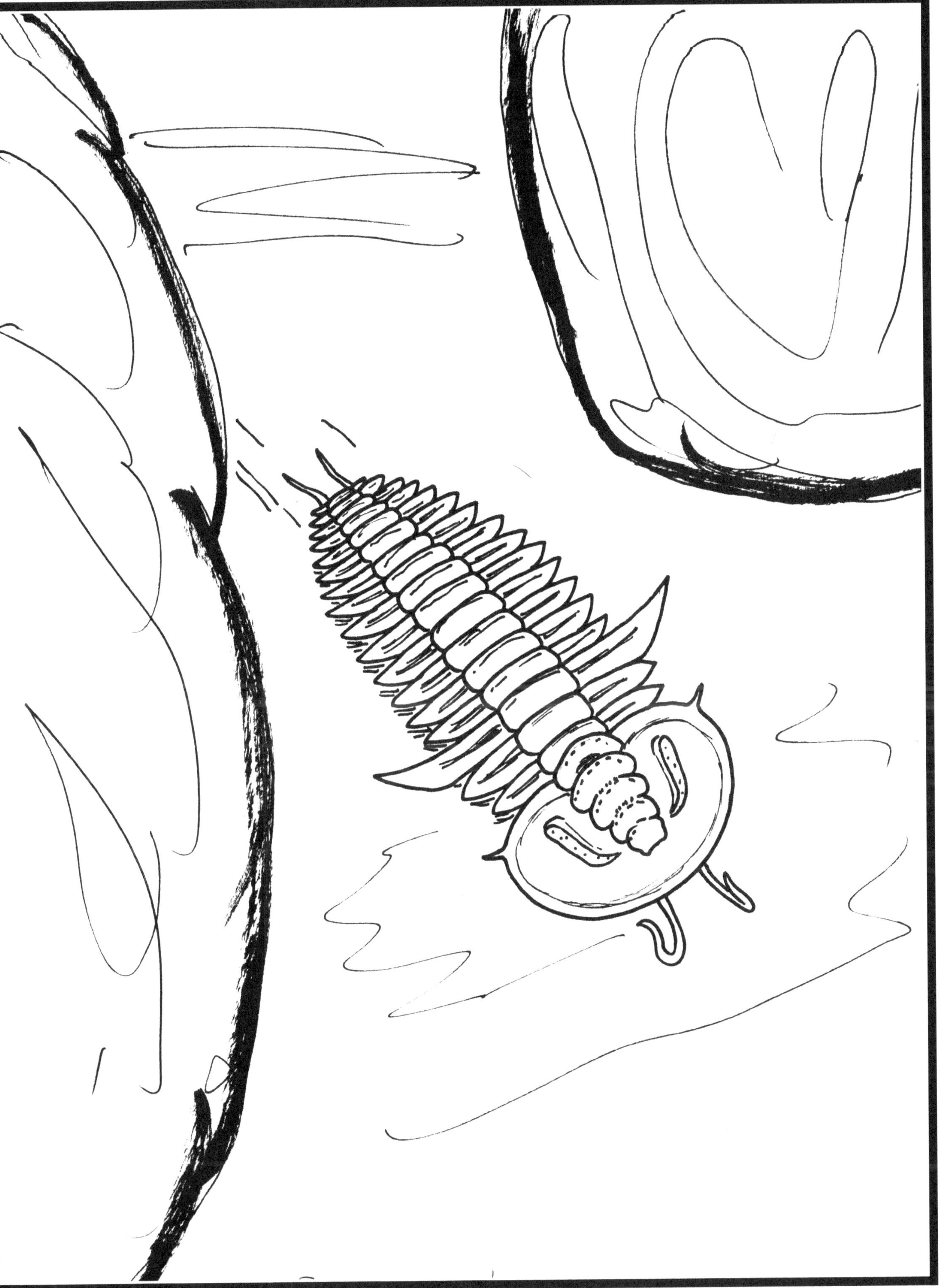

G is for *Galeaspis sphaerica*

Phylum Arthropoda

Class Trilobita

Order Ptychopariida

Family Catillicephalidae

Size Incomplete cranidium about 7 to 12 millimeters wide, complete cephalon perhaps up to 3 centimeters wide.

Time Period Second-third of the Kuyandinian/Franconian/Changshanian Stage of the Late Cambrian, about 495 million years ago.

Location Central Kazakhstan

Comments *Galeaspis sphaerica* is the type species of a genus of ptychopariid trilobites endemic to the Late Cambrian of Kazakhstan, and is most closely related to the genus *Theodenisia*. As trilobites go, species of *Galeaspis* are fairly unremarkable, having proportionally large, helmet, or in the case of *G. sphaerica*, globe-shaped glabella, and probably lead the stereotypical bottom-dwelling lifestyle, scratching out small animals and detritus to devour.

ƕ is for *Han solo*

Phylum	Arthropoda
Class	?Trilobita
Order	Agnostida
Family	Diplagnostidae
Size	About one centimeter in length
Time Period	Middle Ordovician
Location	Zitai Formation in Taoyuan County, Hunan Province, China
Comments	

Han solo, the so-called "Star Wars Trilobite," is an agnostid trilobite from the Middle Ordovician of what is now Hunan Province.

According to the paper by Sam Turvey, the generic name commemorates the Han ethnic group, and the specific name refers to how this is the last and youngest known diplagnostid agnostid. Elsewhere, Turvey would brag about how he named it after Harrison Ford's character on a dare. The presence of Turvey's flippant sense of humor is reinforced when it is noted that, in the same paper, he named another agnostid found in the same area after the pair of heckling Muppets, Waldorf and Statler, ala *Geragnostus statlerwaldorfi*, due to the pygidium resembling their faces.

I is for *Isotelus rex*

Phylum	Arthropoda
Class	Trilobita
Order	Asaphida
Family	Asaphidae
Size	Up to 72 centimeters in length
Time Period	Richmondian Stage of the Cincinnatian Epoch, Late Ordovician, from 449 to 445 million years ago
Location	Churchill River Group, Northern Manitoba
Comments	*Isotelus rex* is the largest trilobite known from intact specimens, and, so far, is the largest known trilobite, period, known from fragments and whole specimens found in marine limestone of Northern Manitoba. Related species are found in Quebec, Ontario and the northeastern United States (especially in Ohio).

I. rex lived in a shallow-water marine environment near the shore, and, according to its size, and fossilized evidence of its relatives' behavior, was probably a worm-hunting predator that dug out prey hidden in the substrate.

J is for *Jujuyaspis keideli*

Phylum Arthropoda

Class Trilobita

Order Ptychopariida

Family Olenidae

Size About up to 3 centimeters in length.

Time Period Early Tremadocian Stage of the Early Ordovician, 485 million years ago.

Location Casa Colorada Formation, aka "Purmamarca Shales," Purmamarca, Jujuy Province, Argentina

Comments *Jujuyaspis keideli* is an Argentinian species of a worldwide genus of ptychopariid trilobites that temporally straddled the Cambrian-Ordovician boundary. The genus is named after Jujuy Province, where the first specimens were found.

J. keideli lived in a deep-water environment suggestive of being near the edge of the continental shelf. Its small eyes are apparently adaptations to this situation.

Related species are found in similarly aged formations in Norway, North America, and Korea.

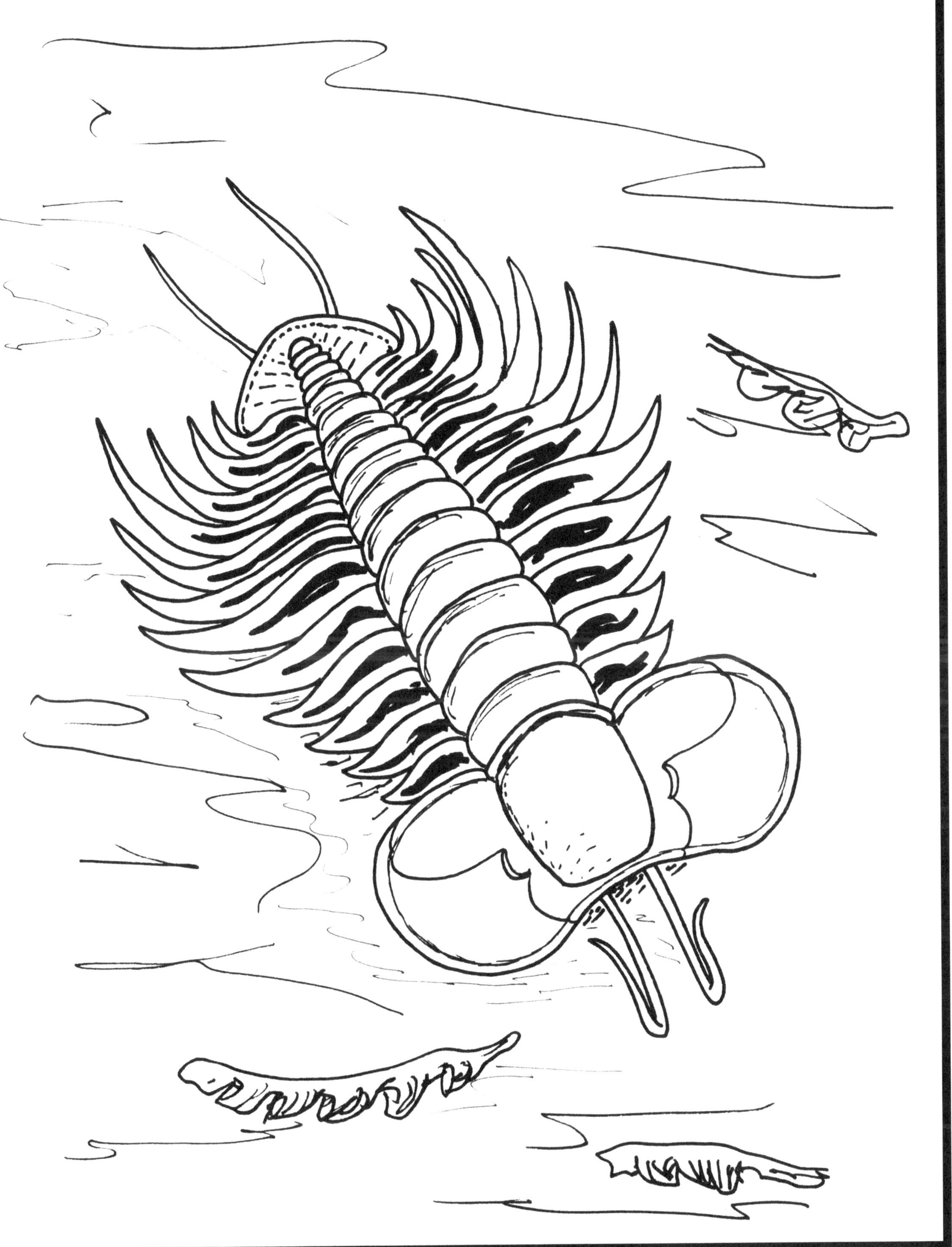

<table>
<tr><td>**K is for**</td><td>*Kleptothule ramusseni*</td></tr>
</table>

Phylum	Arthropoda
Class	Trilobita
Order	Redlichiida
Family	? Nevadiidae
Size	Up to 3 centimeters in length
Time Period	Late Atdabanian of the Early Cambrian Period, from 523 to 518 million years ago
Location	Buen Formation, Sirius Passet, Greenland
Comments	

Kleptothule ramusseni is a bizarre trilobite, even by trilobite standards. *K. ramusseni* superficially resembles a flattened millipede, with a thorax composed of no less than 27 segments, and a fan-like pygidium composed of 5 to 6 segements fused together.

K. ramusseni is from the Early Cambrian Sirius Passet Fauna, a deep sea community in what is now Greenland, and coexisted with worms, primitive arthropods, other trilobites, and the vetulicolian *Ooedigera*, shown here.

The closest relative of *K. ramusseni* is probably the Early Cambrian trilobite, *Nevadia*.

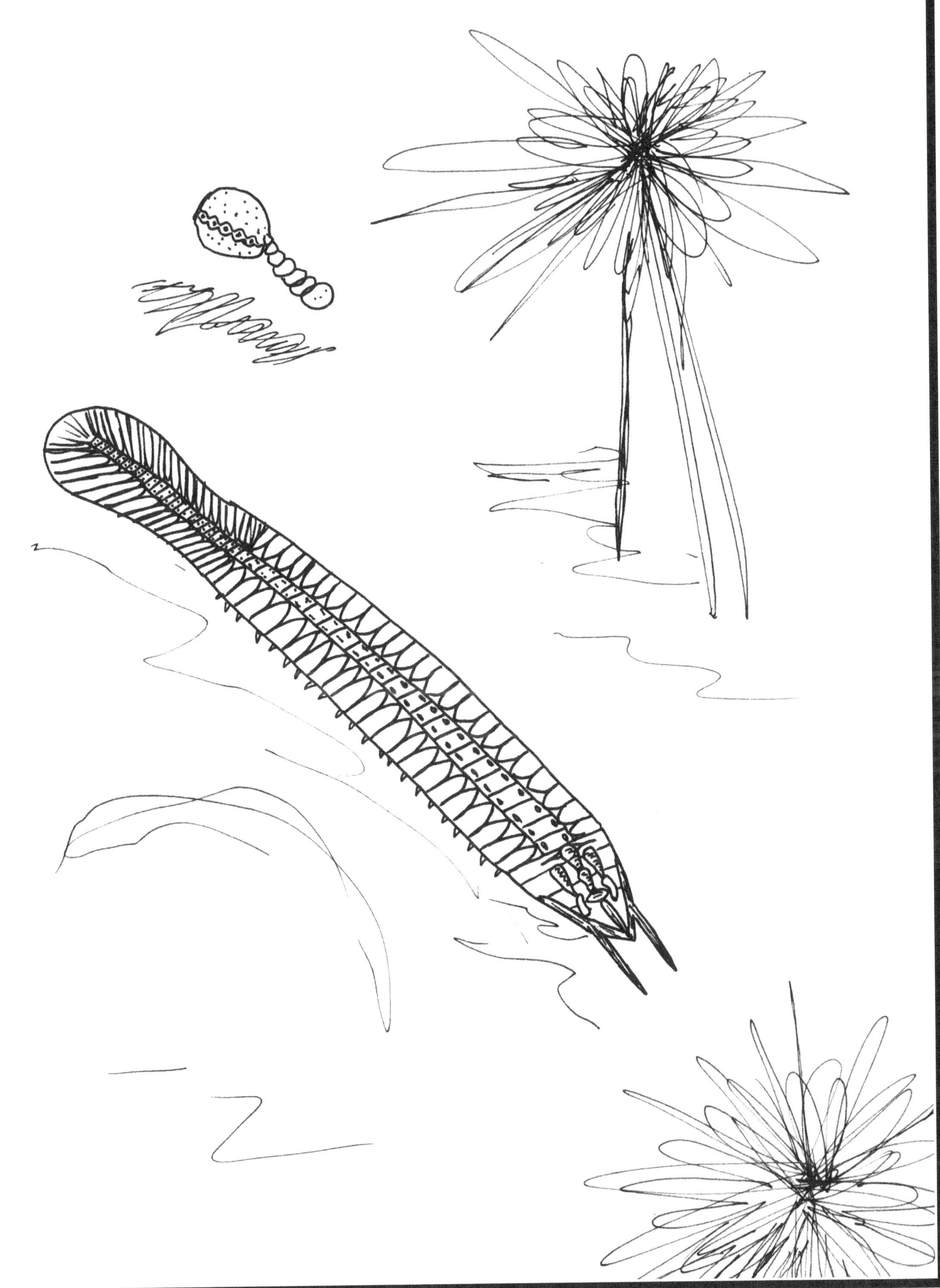

L is for   *Lichas laciniatus*

Phylum   Arthropoda

Class   Trilobita

Order   Lichida

Family   Lichidae

Size   Known from fragments, estimated bodylength maybe 5 centimeters

Time Period Late Ordovician

Location   Baltic coast of Sweden

Comments   The lichids of the genus *Lichas* are found in marine strata from the Late Ordovician until the Middle Silurian of Europe, North America, and Morocco. The genus, together with the family and the order, is named after either a Spartan who allegedly discovered the remains of Orestes, or a servant of Heracles.

Lichids are closely related to the odontopleurids, and some experts group the latter into the former, noting how the two groups diverged during late Cambrian, but still preserved several anatomical similarities.

Lichas laciniatus is known from Late Ordovician-aged marine strata from the Swedish coast of what is now the Baltic Sea. Thus far, it is only known from fragments, though, other species, such as *L. marocanus* from Morocco, are known from complete specimens. Lichids, including *L. laciniatus*, are thought to have all crawled along the substrate and gobbled up whatever smaller animals they could find and catch.

ℳ is for *Malchi magnificus*

Phylum	Arthropoda
Class	Trilobita
Order	Proetida
Family	Phillipsiidae
Size	About 2 to 4 centimeters long.
Time Period	Late Tournaisian Epoch of the Lower Carboniferous Period, about 346 to 345 million years ago.
Location	Malchi Formation of the Rockhampton Group at Malchi Creek, west of Rockhampton, Queensland, Australia
Comments	During the Late Devonian, trilobites began a decline in diversity, with the various Devonian groups, Odontopleura, Lichiida, Harpetida, Corynexochida, Phacopida, and Proetida slowly dying out, one by one, until only the Proetids survive beyond the Hangenberg Event of the Late Devonian Extinction.

During the Carboniferous, the surviving proetids began slowly rediversifying. The phillipsiid proetid, *Malchi magnificus*, named for Malchi Creek, where the first fossil specimens were found, was a part of a diversity of Eastern Australian trilobites that arose soon after the end of the Devonian. Here, the larger *Malchi* is compared with the related *Planokaskia gibsoni* (which is actually from New South Wales).

N is for *Neodrepanura premesnili*

Phylum Arthropoda

Class Trilobita

Order Odontopleurida

Family Damsellidae

Size Around 6 centimeters in length

Time Period Guzhangian Epoch of the Late Cambrian, 501 to 497 million years ago

Location Kushan Formation of Shandong Province, China

Comments *Neodrepanura premesnili* is the best known species of the genus *Neodrepanura,* a genus of odontopleurid trilobites of the family Damesellidae.

The pygidia of many Chinese trilobites are called "swallow stones," 燕子石 (yanzi shi), or "bat stones," 蝙蝠石 (bianfu shi), named so for their resemblance to a swallow or a bat in flight. Swallow stones and bat stones have been in Chinese culture as good luck charms and as herbal medicine for centuries.

N. premesnili is the first of these swallowstone trilobites studied by Europeans, being first described as *"Drepanura" premesnili* in 1899. However, even though this trilobite has been known, sort of, to the Chinese for thousands of years, and to the Europeans for over 110 years, the first intact specimen of these trilobites was only discovered in 2011. Other recent discoveries about *N. premesnili* include an examination of the hyponome (shown here in the lower right corner), which is a mouthguard-like plate, the size and proportions of which suggests a carnivorous diet.

O is for   *Odontopleura ovalis*

Phylum   Arthropoda

Class   Trilobita

Order   Odontopleurida

Family   Odontopleuridae

Size   Up to 3 centimeters long, not including spines.

Time Period Wenloch Epoch of the Middle Silurian, about 425 million years ago

Location   Liteň Formation in Loděnice, Czech Republic, and Gotland, of Sweden.

Comments   *Odontopleura ovata* is the type species of the order Odontopleurida, and embodies the odontopleurids' reputation for grandiose spinosity among trilobites. The genus name literally translates as "teeth-ribs," can either refer to the way the spines come off of the pleura or segments like fangs, or how the arrangement of spines make the animal look like the horrible jaw of a monster with rib-like teeth.

The original purpose of the odontopleurids' exaggerated spininess is a popular subject of speculation in evolutionary biology. The most obvious conclusion is that the spines detered bigmouthed gnathostome vertebrate predators from swallowing or biting their odontopleurid owners. While this is a reasonable deduction for Silurian and Devonian odontopleurids, it falls apart when one realizes that the odontopleurids first evolved their extravagent armament during the Ordovician, before the advent of gnathostomes. Other ideas suggested include spreading the weight of the animal in order to prevent it from sinking into mud, or allow encrusting organisms to grow on them in order to better disguise themselves.

O. ovata is known from Wenlock-aged marine strata in Bohemia and Gotland.

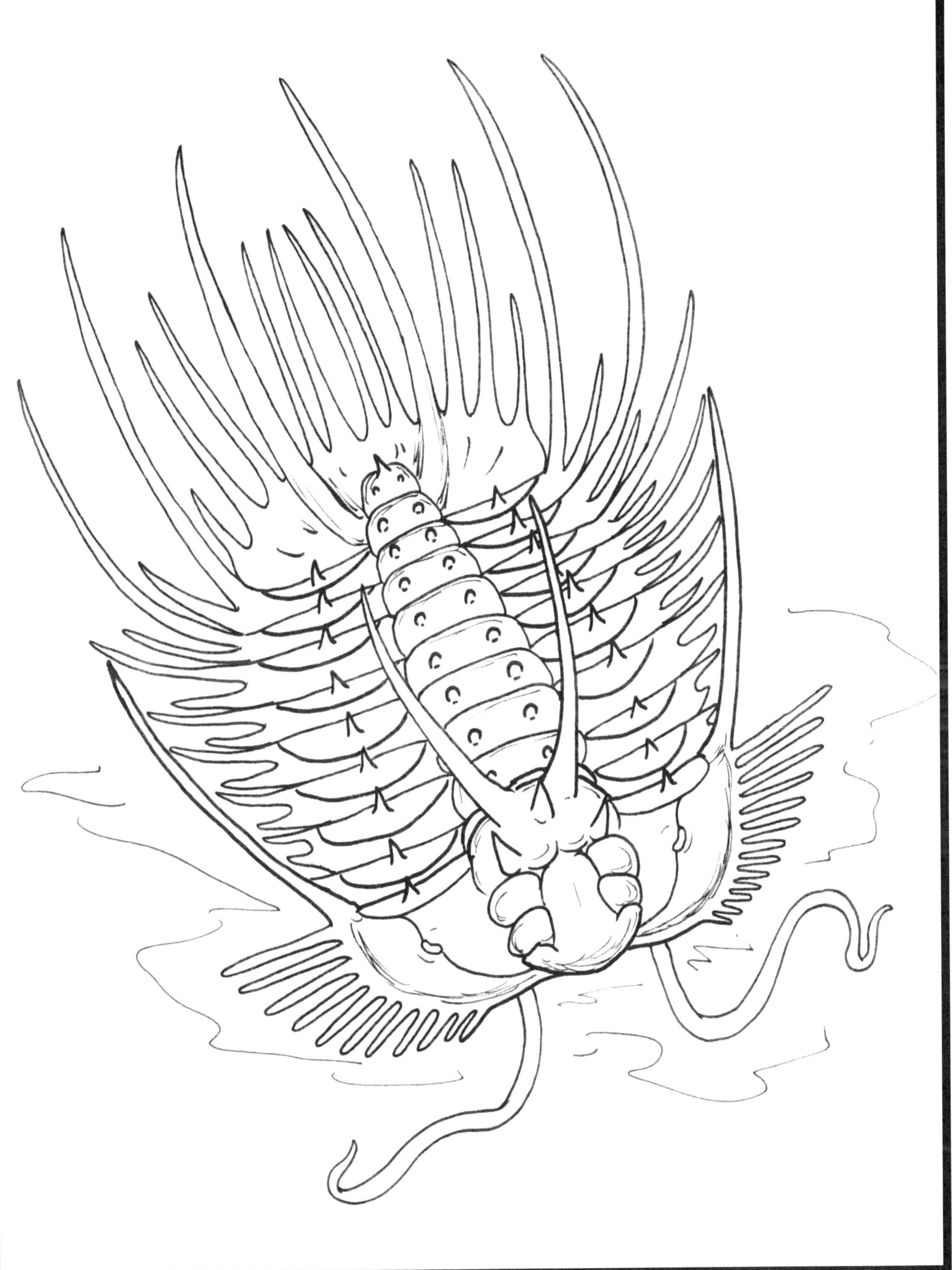

P is for *Paradoxides paradoxissimus*

Phylum	Arthropoda
Class	Trilobita
Order	Redlichiida
Family	Paradoxididae
Size	Specimens range in size from 10 to 20 centimeters in length
Time Period	"Series 2" of the Middle Cambrian, 513 to 501 million years ago
Location	Scandinavia

Comments

Paradoxides paradoxissimus is a large Cambrian trilobite, and is the type species of the iconic Cambrian genus *Paradoxides*. Species of *Paradoxides* lived primarily off the coast of what was once the island continent of Avalonia, in the Iapetus Ocean: today, this corresponds to the regions of Northeastern North America, Western Europe, and Morocco. *P. paradoxissimus*, originally described by Wahlenberg as "*Entomostracites paradoxissimus*," lived in what would become modern-day Scandinavia. Adult specimens of *P. paradoxissimus* have 21 segments. This species, as with other members of the genus, are thought to have been benthic, crawling predators that ate any smaller animal they could find on or dig out of the substrate.

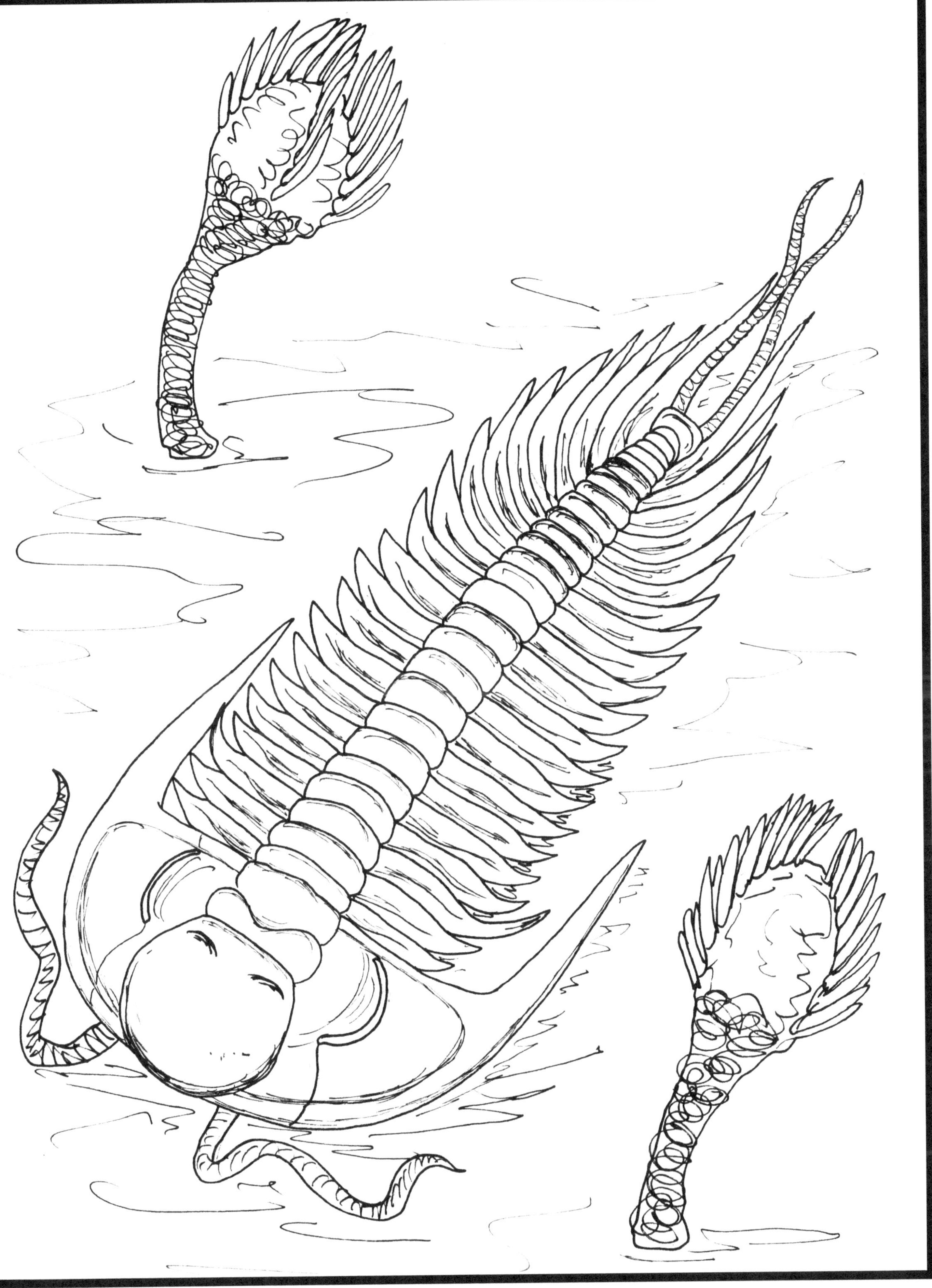

Q is for *Quitacetra arenata*

Phylum	Arthropoda
Class	Trilobita
Order	Ptychopariida
Family	Mapaniidae
Size	Incomplete cranidia about 13 millimeters wide, complete cephalon maybe up to 30 to 40 millimeters wide.
Time Period	Mindyallan division of the Early Furongian Epoch of the Late Cambrian, about 497 million years ago
Location	Steamboat Sandstone of Quita Creek, Mindyallan, (Northwestern) Queensland
Comments	*Quitacetra arenata* is a small ptychopariid trilobite from the Early Furongian Epoch of Late Cambrian Queensland, where it was an Australian representative of an otherwise primarily Chinese trilobite family, Mapaniidae, in a diverse, species-abundant community of trilobites. This trilobite community lived in a sandy bottomed environment, which the epithet *arenata* partially refers to (it also refers to the small-grained texture of *Quitacetra*'s shell, too).

R is for *Redlichia noeltingi*

Phylum Arthropoda

Class Trilobita

Order Redlichiida

Family Redlichiidae

Size Cephalon is 2 to 3 centimeters wide

Time Period Late Canglangpuian or "Cambrian Stage 4" of the Early Cambrian, about 510 to 509 million years ago

Location Salt Formation of Western Pakistan

Comments *Redlichia noeltingi* is the type species of the wide-ranging type genus of the primitive trilobite order Redlichiida. *R. noeltingi* is from Early Cambrian-aged marine strata in the Salt Range in Western Pakistan (not to be confused with the Salt Formation in France). Other members of *Redlichia* are found in similarly aged marine strata of Southern and Western China, Korea, Iran, Spain, Siberia, Australia and Antarctica.

Redlichiid trilobites are the most anatomically primitive trilobites, and are thought to be ancestral to all other trilobites, except, perhaps, the naraoiids and the agnostids, provided these two groups are eventually unequivocally proven to not be trilobites.

<table>
<tr><td>S is for</td><td>Shumardia granulosa</td></tr>
</table>

Phylum	Arthropoda
Class	Trilobita
Order	Ptychopariida
Family	Shumardiidae
Size	Large adult maybe up to 3 millimeters in length
Time Period	Perhaps Latest Cambrian to Early Tremadocian of the Early Ordovician
Location	Northeastern North America

Comments

Shumardia granulosa is the type species of a large genus of tiny ptychopariid trilobites found in marine strata of North America and Europe from the Middle Cambrian to Early Ordovician: *S. granulosa* is found primarily in Quebec, and New York, in strata from the Cambrian-Ordovician boundary. Species of *Shumardia* have no eyes, and apparently grubbed around in sediment to hunt for nourishing detritus, as were and did their relatives, including the even tinier, 1 millimeter long *Acanthopleurella* of Early Ordovician England.

The first specimens of *Shumardia* were originally thought to be those of an agnostid, then, later, much suspicion remained (for a while) that these were larval or embryonic forms of other, larger trilobites. The geologist, Sir James "Stubbie" Stubblefield studied numerous specimens of *Shumardia* throughout his long and illustrious career. In 1926, he demonstrated the life history of this trilobite, and, in doing so, demonstrated how trilobites produce more segments as they grew. This was done by, during a molt, having the pygidium "release" the anteriormost segment into the thorax as the other thoracic segments are then shuffled headwards. This process would then be repeatedly demonstrated by other researchers in other related and unrelated trilobites.

$\mathcal{T}$ **is for** *Terataspis grandis*

Phylum Arthropoda

Class Trilobita

Order Lichida

Family Lichidae

Size Unknown, fragments suggest an animal up to 60 centimeters long.

Time Period End of the Emsian Epoch, Early Devonian, about 397 million years ago

Location Schoharie-Bois Formation, Tri-State Area, New York, United States, and Ontario, Canada.

Comments *Terataspis grandis* is the third largest known trilobite. Although *T. grandis* is currently only known from fragments of molted exoskeleton, enough of these pieces, together with intact specimens of relatives, enough material is known to confidently estimate an average adult length of around 60 centimeters.

So far, *T. grandis* is dwarfed only by species of the related genus *Uralichas sp*, individuals of which had an average length of 66 centimeters, and the giant Ordovician-aged asaphid, *Isotelus rex*, which is up to a whopping 77 centimeters in average length.

Terataspis was probably a detritivore, but, given its enormous size and large glabellum, it was probably also an opportunistic predator that ate whatever smaller animal it could dig up, including worms, molluscs, and, smaller arthropods. Whether it could have eaten trilobites like the individuals of the phacopid, *Phacops rana,* shown here with it, is currently unknown, however.

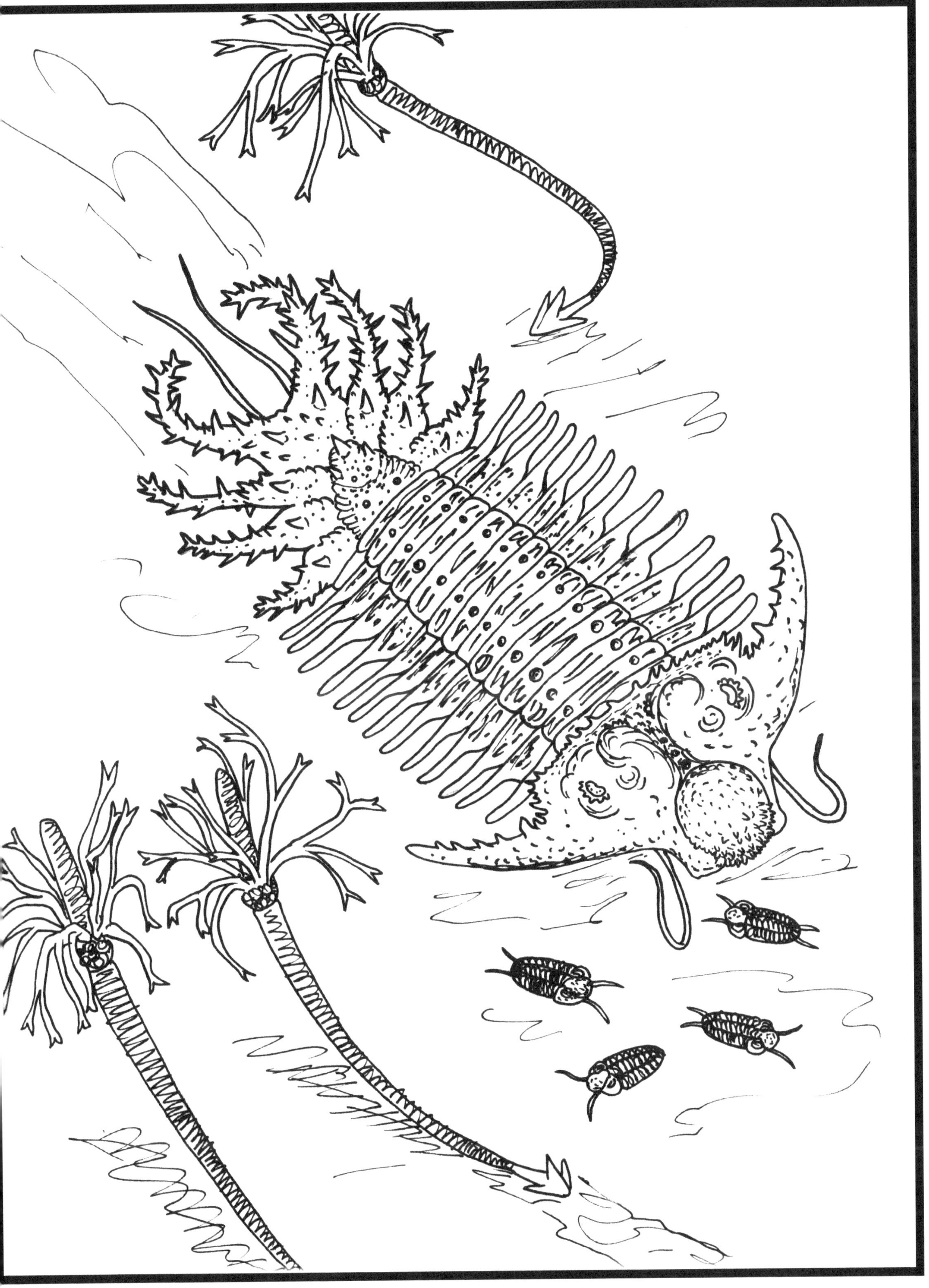

U is for   *Utaspis marjumensis*

Phylum   Arthropoda

Class   Trilobita

Order   Ptychopariida

Family   Alokistocaridae

Size   About 2.5 to 9 centimeters long

Time Period   "Stage 5" of the Middle Cambrian, 507 million years ago.

Location   Wheeler Shale Formation and Marjum Formation, Millard County, Utah

Comments   *Utaspis marjumensis* is a large ptychopariid trilobite that is a rare to uncommon fossil in the Wheeler Shale and Marjum Formations in Utah. *U. marjumensis'* anatomy demonstrates that it is a descendant of the "stone waterbug" trilobites of genus *Elrathia*, several species of which are also found in the Wheeler Shale and Marjum Formations. This suggests that *Utaspis* was a member of a local diversification *Elrathia* diversification event.

V is for *Validaspis judomica*

Phylum Arthropoda

Class Trilobita

Order Ptychopariida

Family Palaeolenidae

Size Estimated length maybe 1 to 2 centimeters

Time Period Early Botomian Stage of "Stage 4" of the Cambrian Period, 524 million years ago

Location Petrotsvet Formation, Siberian Platform, Russia

Comments *Validaspis judomica* is a primitive ptychopariid trilobite from the Early Cambrian of Siberia, when the whole area was a series of tropical to subtropical reefs made of accumulated mounds of shells, sponges and coralline algae.

V. judomica, and other species of *Validaspis* are closely related to the ptychopariid genus *Palaeolenus*, differing in the architecture of the glabella.

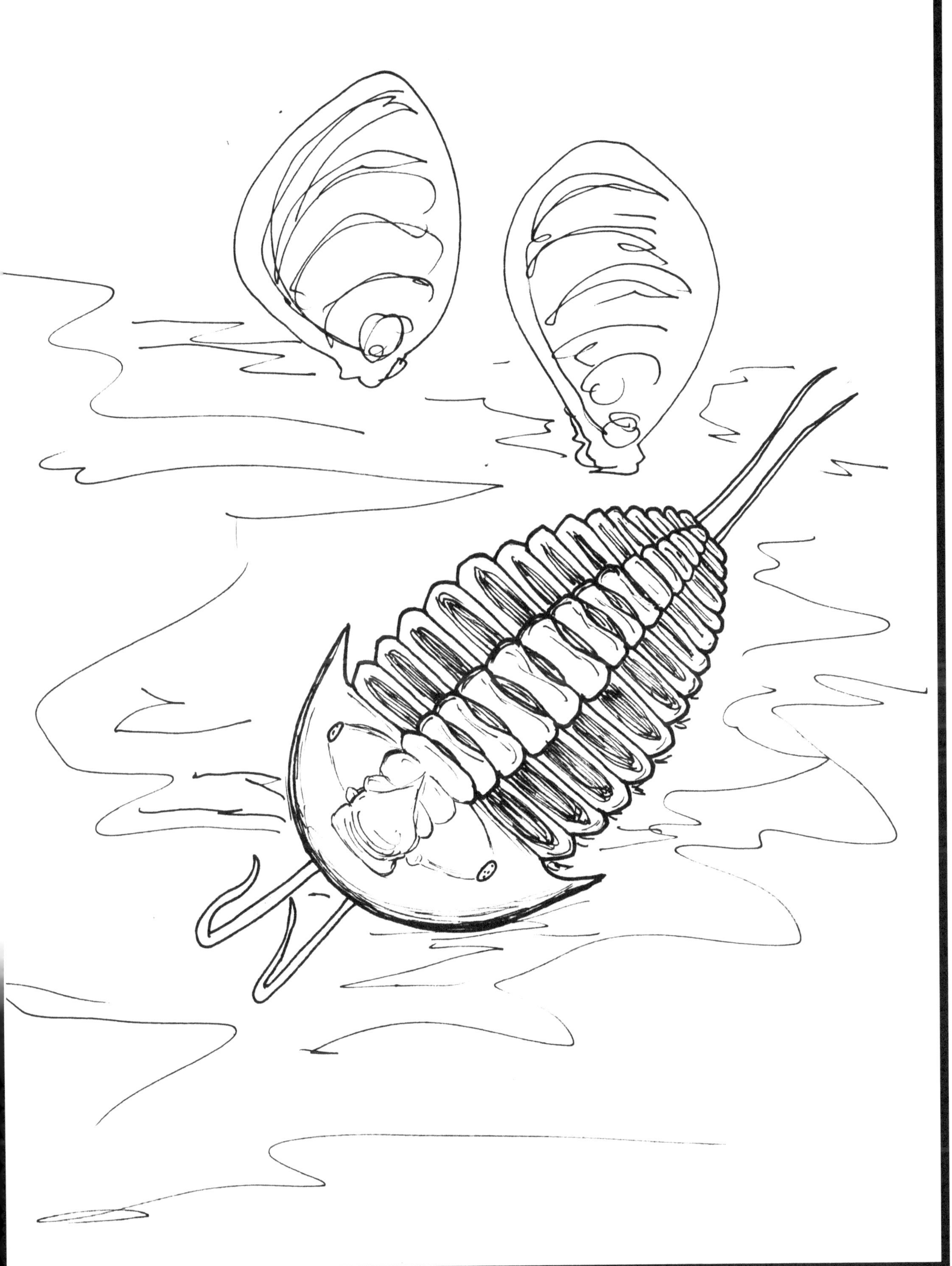

W is for   *Walliserops sp.*

Phylum	Arthropoda
Class	Trilobita
Order	Phacopida
Family	Acastidae
Size	Average bodylength without trident about 3 centimeters
Time Period	Upper Emsian Epoch to the Lower Eifelian Epoch, of the Early to Middle Devonian.
Location	Morocco
Comments	The story of the "Trident Trilobites" of *Walliserops* is a weird and sordid tale, from us, humans' point of view. When the first species (the lower three, long-stemmed individuals, *W. trifurcatus*, in this picture) was described, the purpose of its trident was a peculiar mystery. When a second variety with a short-stemmed trident was found (i.e., the upper right one, which is now described as *W. tridens*), researchers were all "Hooray! The first blatant example of sexual dimorphism in trilobites!"

Of course, very few things in paleontology are rarely ever so blatantly clear-cut, especially when a third variety, then a fourth variety were discovered, showing that, instead of one species with two distinct lengths of tridents, there was a cluster of at least six different species, each with its own distinct trident (like, for example, the individual with a spork-like trident, *W. lindoei)*. Aside from helping individuals identify which species other individual tridentibites belonged to, the primary function of the trident continues to elude researchers.

Further compounding this weirdness is the fact that, with the species *W. trifurcatus*, individuals often had forks that bent assymetrically to one side: the reason for this, too, eludes researchers.

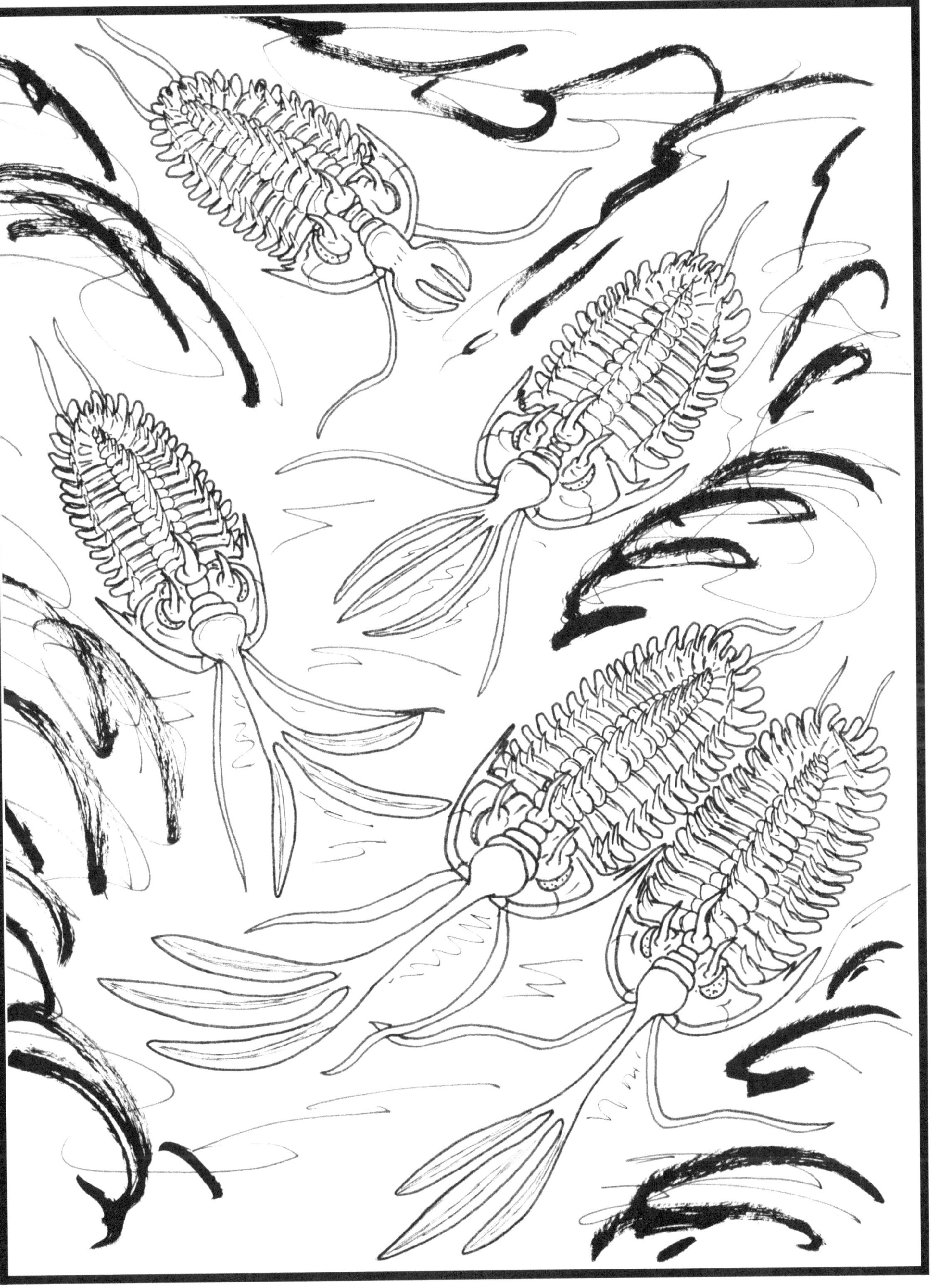

X is for *Xiuqiella rectangulata*

Phylum	Arthropoda
Class	Trilobita
Order	Corynexochida
Family	Chengkouiidae
Size	Adult may be up to 2 centimeters in length
Time Period	Nangaoian Stage of the later Cambrian Stage 3, 516 to 513 million years ago.
Location	Yingzuiyan Formation, Chengkou, near Chongqingu, China.
Comments	*Xiuqiella rectangulata* is a rare corynexochid trilobite from the Cambrian of (what is now) Southwestern China, known from fragments, primarily of a rectangular-shaped glabellum.

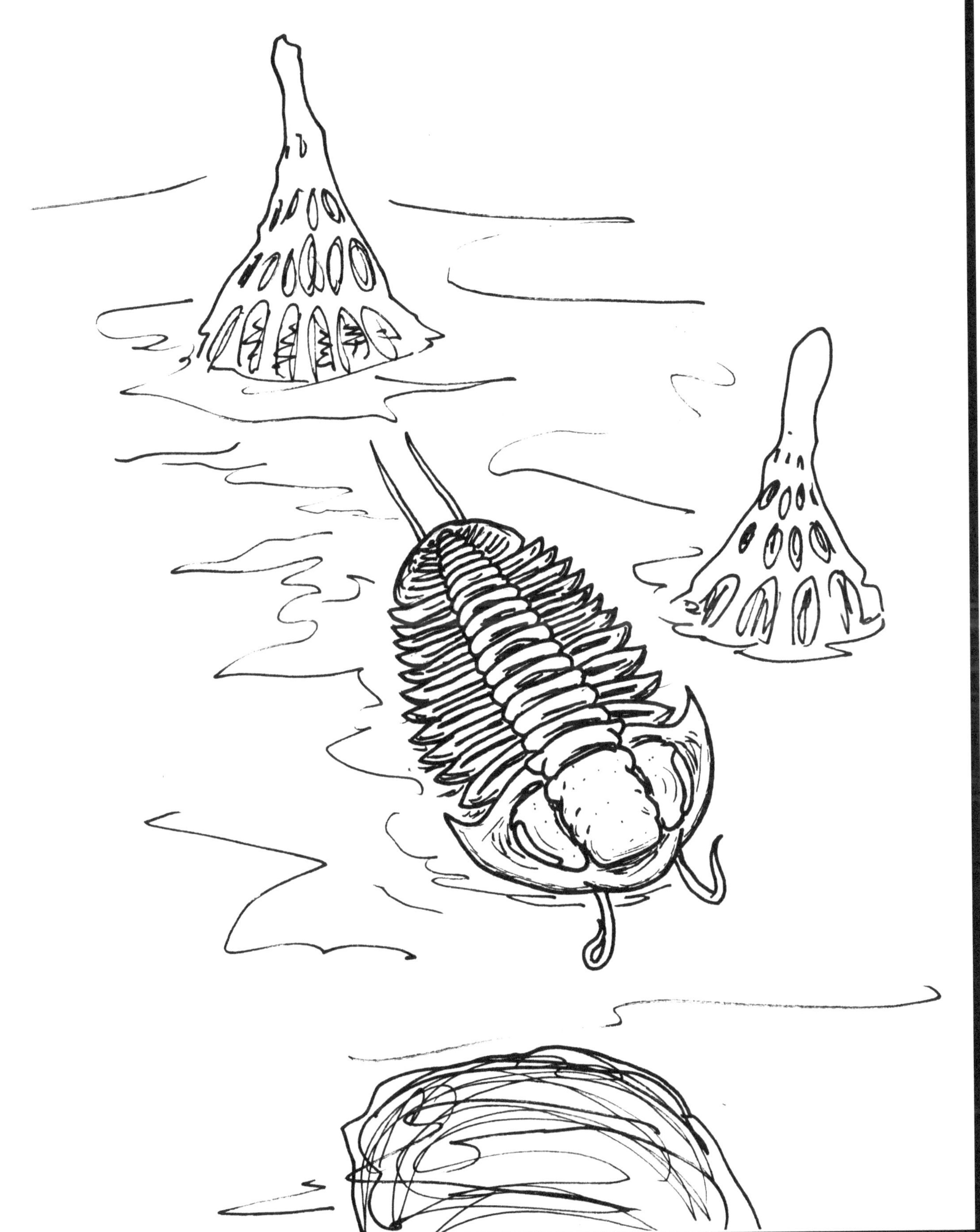

Y is for *Yunnanocephalus yunnanensis*

Phylum Arthropoda

Class Trilobita

Order Ptychopariida

Family Yunnanocephalidae

Size Length of adults up to 2 centimeters

Time Period "Stage 3" of the Cambrian Period, 515 million years ago

Location Chengjiang County, Yunnan Province, China

Comments *Yunnanocephalus yunnanensis* is a small ptychopariid trilobite, and is one of the more common trilobites of the Chengjiang Fauna. Its unusual appearance, with a cephalon with rounded genal corners, has lead researchers to reappraise its taxonomic position several times. When it was originally discovered, it was described as a member of the genus *Ptychoparia*. Later, it would be taken out of that genus, and placed in its own unique genus (as "*Yunnanocephalus*") within Order Redlichiida before it would be returned to Ptychopariida.

Other species of *Yunnanocephalus* are found in similarly aged marine strata of Australia and Antarctica.

Z is for *Zacanthoides romingeri*

Phylum   Arthropoda

Order   Corynexochida

Family   Zacanthoididae

Size   Length up to 3.5 centimeters

Time Period "Stage 3" of the Cambrian Period, 508 million years ago

Location   Mount Stephen and Burgess Shale, British Columbia, Spencer Shale, Utah.

Comments   *Zacanthoides romingeri* is one of several trilobites from the famous Burgess Shale community in Cambrian-aged British Columbia. Fossils of this spinose, thorny-looking corynexochid are also found in slightly younger marine strata in Utah: related species are found throughout Middle Cambrian marine strata in North America and Greenland.

Zacanthoides romingeri was originally described as "*Embolimus spinosa*" in 1887 by geologist Carl Rominger from specimens given to him by his friend and fellow geologist, Otto Klotz. The next year, geologist Charles Walcott noted that "*Embolimus*" was already in use as a synonym of *Embolemus,* a genus of British parasitoid wasps, as he revised Rominger's work in conjunction with describing trilobites he found in Nevada. Walcott would rename "*Embolimus spinosa*" as *Zacanthoides.* As a peace offering, Walcott would name the Burgess Shale/Mount Stephen *Zacanthoides* after Rominger, while he appropriated the epithet *spinosa* to name the Nevada *Zacanthoides* as *Z. spinosus.*

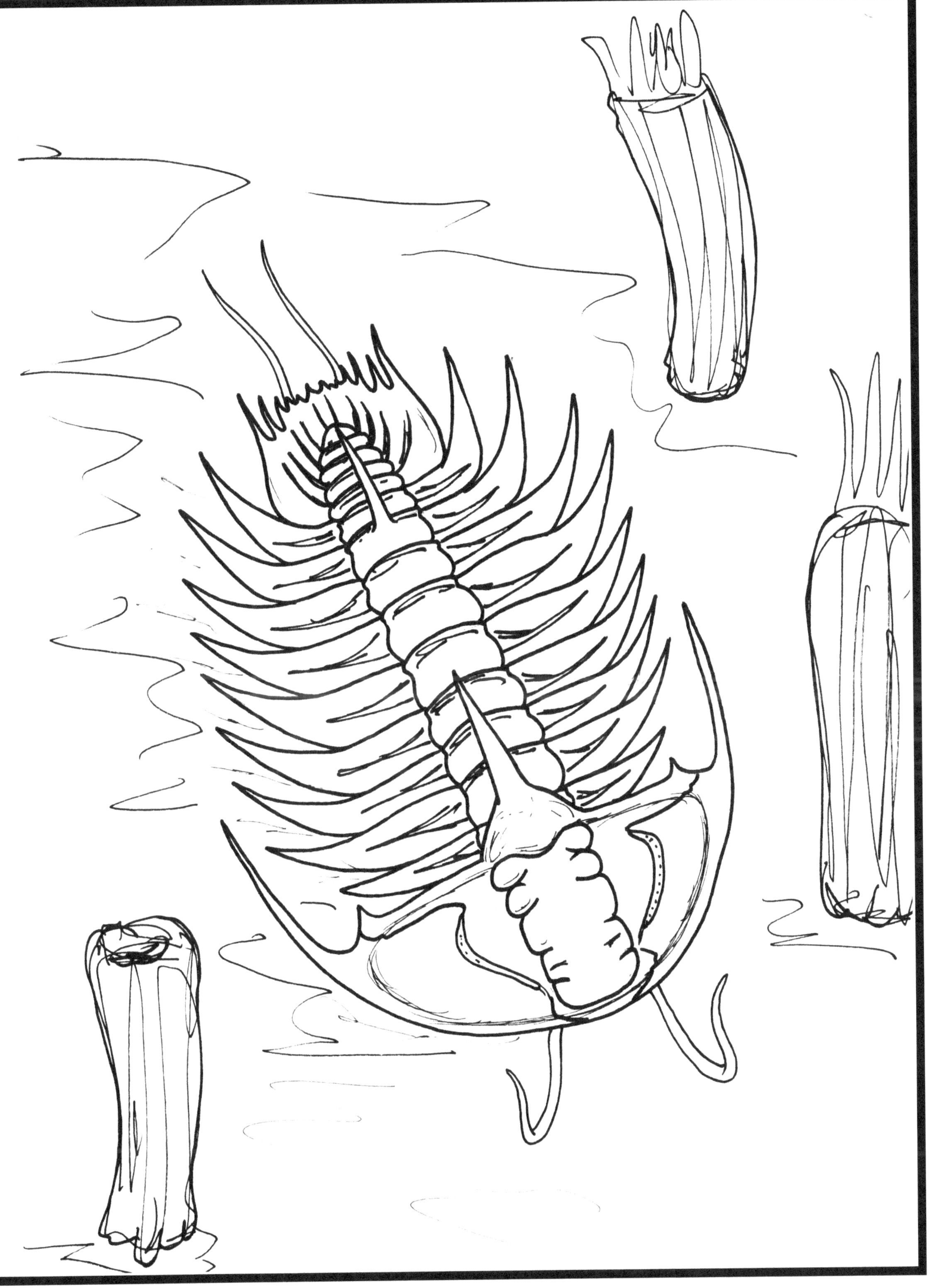

Bibliography

- ALBERTI, G. K. B. 1983. Trilobiten des ju¨ngeren Siluriums sowie des Unterund Mittel-Devons IV. Senckenbergiana lethaea, 64
- Astashkin, Vladimir A., and Alekseĭ IUrʹevich Rozanov. *The Cambrian system on the Siberian platform: correlation chart and explanatory notes*. No. 27. International Union of Geological Sciences, 1991.
- Basse, M., 2010. Neue und wenig bekannte Taxa der Scutelluinae, Proetinae und Otarioninae (Trilobita) aus dem Mitteldevon der Blankenheim-, Hillesheim- und Prüm-Mulde (Eifel). Dortmunder Beiträge zur Landeskunde, Naturwissenschaftliche Mitteilungen, 42, 75-119.
- Borowski T. Odontopleura generalandersi - a new Silurian trilobite species of the Odontopleura genus occurring in the north Poland. Curr World Environ 2008;3(2):213-216.
- Calner, Mikael, et al. "The first record of Odontopleura ovata (Trilobita) from Scandinavia: part of a middle Silurian intercontinental shelly benthos mass occurrence." GFF 128.1 (2006): 33-37.
- Chatterton, Brian DE, and Stacey Gibb. "Latest Early to Early Middle Devonian Trilobites from the Erbenochile Bed, Jbel Issoumour, Southeastern Morocco." *Journal of Paleontology* 84.6 (2010): 1188-1205.
- Dai, Tao, and Xingliang Zhang. "Ontogeny of the trilobite Yunnanocephalus yunnanensis from the Chengjiang lagerstätte, lower Cambrian, southwest China." *Alcheringa* 32.4 (2008): 465-468.
- Engel, B. A., and N. Morris. "Ditomopyginae (Trilobita) from the Lower Carboniferous of eastern Australia (i) Australokaskia (Australokaskia), Planokaskia, Malchi n. gen." *Geologica et Palaeontologica* 28 (1994): 79-101.
- Fortey, Richard. *Trilobite: eyewitness to evolution*. Vintage, 2010.
- Hollingsworth, JStewart. "Fallotaspidoid trilobite assemblage (Lower Cambrian) from the Esmeralda Basin (western Nevada, USA): The oldest trilobites from Laurentia." *Memoirs of the Association of Australasian Palaeontologists* 33 (2007): 123.
- Ivshin, N. K. *Upper Cambrian trilobites of Kazakhstan*. Amerind, 1955 (English translation) 1983.
- Jago, James Bernard, et al. "A review of the Cambrian biostratigraphy of South Australia." *Palaeoworld* 15.3-4 (2006): 406-423.
- Kloc, Gerald J. "Spine function in the odontopleurid trilobites Leonaspis and Dicranurus from the Devonian of Oklahoma." *The Paleontological Society Special Publications* 6 (1992): 167-167.
- KOBAYASHI, Teiichi, and Takashi HAMADA. "Advance Reports on the Permian Trilobites of Japan. I." *Proceedings of the Japan Academy, Series B* 58.3 (1982): 45-48.
- 小泉斉. "阿武隈山地・高倉山層群(ペルム紀) のPhillipsiidae 新属三葉虫," *地球科学*26.1 (1972): 19-25.

- Levi-Setti, Riccardo. *TRILOBITES.* University of Chicago Press, 1995.
- Liu, Qing, and Qianping Lei. "First known complete specimen of Neodrepanura (Trilobita: Damesellidae) from the Cambrian Kushan Formation, Shandong, China." Alcheringa: An Australasian Journal of Palaeontology 35.3 (2011): 397-403.
- Ludvigsen, Rolf, ed. *Life in stone: a natural history of British Columbia's fossils.* UBC Press, 2011.
- Moore, R.C. (1959). *Arthropoda I - Arthropoda General Features, Proarthropoda, Euarthropoda General Features, Trilobitomorpha.* <u>Treatise on Invertebrate Paleontology</u>. Part O. Boulder, Colorado/Lawrence, Kansas: Geological Society of America/University of Kansas Press. pp. 1–560. <u>ISBN</u> <u>0-8137-3015-5</u>.
- Öpik, Armin Alexander. *The Mindyallan fauna of north-western Queensland.* Bureau of mineral resources, geology and geophysics, 1967.
- Pack, P. D.; Gayle, H. B. (2009). "A New Olenellid Trilobite, *Biceratops nevadensis*, from the Lower Cambrian near Las Vegas, Nevada". *Journal of Paleontology.* **45** (5). pp. 893–898.
- Peng, S. C. "Historical review of trilobite research in China." Fabulous Fossils—300 years of Worldwide Research on Trilobites. NY State Museum Bulletin, New York State Museum, Albany, New York (2007): 171-191.
- Robison, Richard A. "Late middle Cambrian faunas from western Utah." *Journal of Paleontology* (1964): 510-566.
- Tripp, Ronald Pearson. "The classification and evolution of the superfamily Lichacea (Trilobita)." *Geological Magazine* 94.2 (1957): 104-122.
- Turvey, Samuel T. "Agnostid trilobites from the Arenig–Llanvirn of South China." *Earth and Environmental Science Transactions of The Royal Society of Edinburgh* 95.3-4 (2004): 527-542.
- Whiteley, Thomas Edward, Gerald J. Kloc, and Carlton Elliot Brett. *Trilobites of New York: an illustrated guide.* Ithaca, NY: Cornell University Press, 2002.
- Whittington, H. B.; et al., eds. (1997). *Part O, Revised, Volume 1 – Trilobita – Introduction, Order Agnostida, Order Redlichiida.* <u>Treatise on Invertebrate Paleontology</u>.
- Xian-Guang, Hou, et al. *The Cambrian fossils of Chengjiang, China: the flowering of early animal life.* John Wiley & Sons, 2017.
- W. T. Zhang, Y. H. Lu, Z. L. Zhu, Y. Y. Qian, H. L. Lin, Z. Zhou, S. Zhang and J. L. Yuan. 1980. Cambrian trilobite faunas of southwestern China. *Palaeontologia Sinica, new series B* **16**:1-497 [W. Kiessling/U. Merkel]

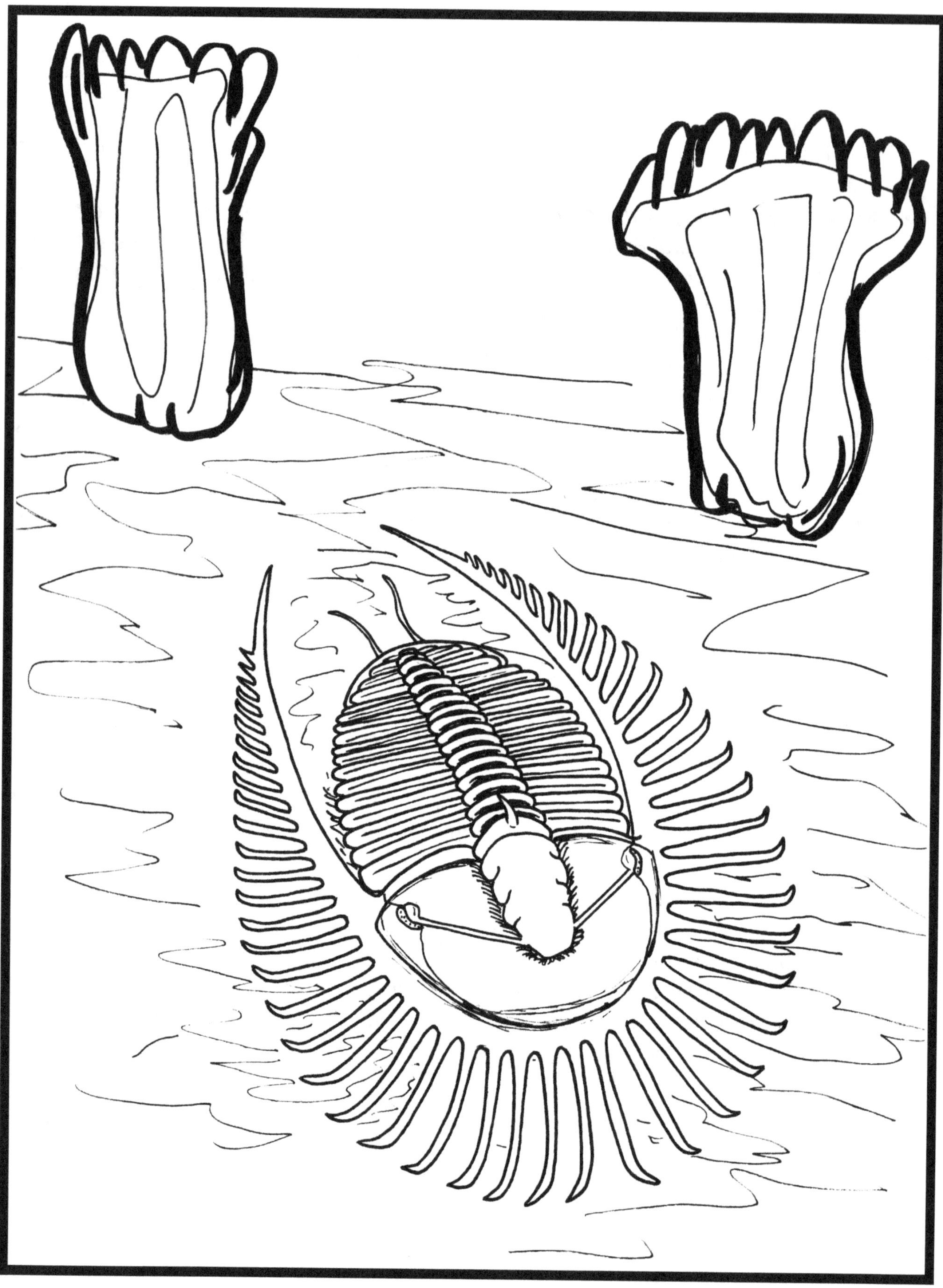

About the Artist

Stanton F. Fink is a student of Biology and Chinese Medicine, and makes a hobby of drawing monsters and researching flowers, arcane-looking creatures, prehistoric animals, fish, reptiles, birds and the occasional, really grotesque fungal fruiting body.

Stanton grew up and went to school in California and is currently living, drawing, and gardening in Oregon.

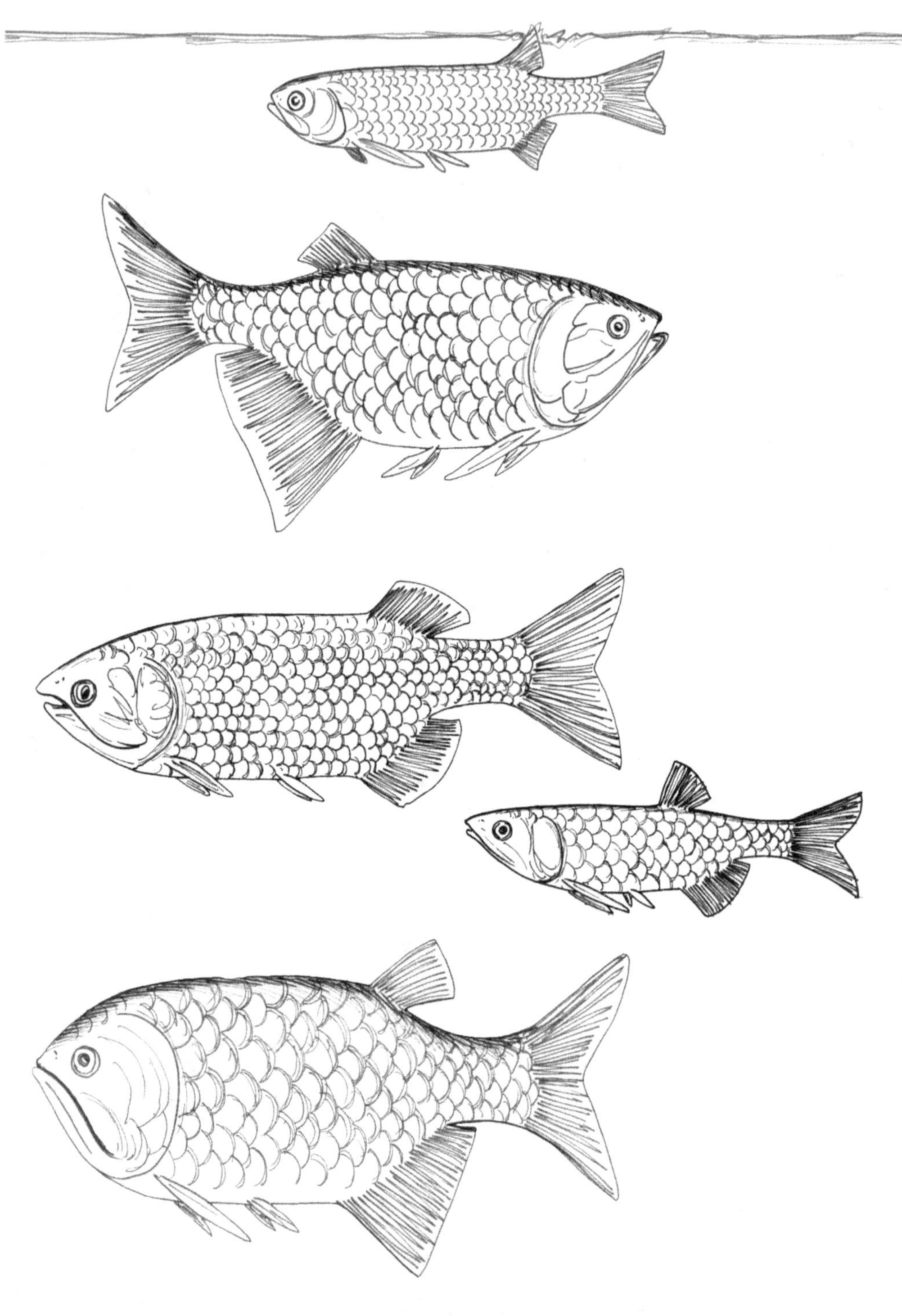